# THE AFRICAN DESERT

# THE AFRICAN DESERT

Bernard Plossu

THE UNIVERSITY OF ARIZONA PRESS
Tucson

## *About the Photographer*

The first photograph that Bernard Plossu took when he arrived in Agadès, Niger, in 1975 was of a group of nomads singing under the moon. This experience prompted his further travels in the deserts of Africa. A Frenchman who lived for some years in Santa Fe, New Mexico, Plossu has had a number of solo and group exhibitions in the United States and in Europe. Major published works include *New Mexico Revisited* and *Le Voyage Méxicain.* His prints are part of several collections, including the Center for Creative Photography, the Amon Carter Museum, George Eastman House, and the Bibliothèque Nationale of France.

All royalties from the sale of *The African Desert* are being donated to CARE for African drought relief.

THE UNIVERSITY OF ARIZONA PRESS



This book was set in Bulmer and Bulmer Italic types.
Manufactured in the U.S.A.

Library of Congress Cataloging-in-Publication Data

Plossu, Bernard.
The African desert.

1. Sahara — Description and travel — Views. I. Title.
DT333.P62 1987 966 87-5021
ISBN 0-8165-0934-4 (pbk. : alk. paper)

British Library Cataloguing in Publication data are available.

*Only in the desert could a man find freedom.*

(saying of Bedu tribes as told by Wilfred Thesiger in *Arabian Sands*)

*They pass by, silent, wearing their mourning veils in the mineral whiteness of the streets. . . .*

(The Renegade, *Exile and the Kingdom,* Albert Camus)

*. . . and beyond was the inevitable horizon of the desert*

(*The Sheltering Sky,* Paul Bowles)

# Preface

*Modern man is forever barred from the full experience of the many sensory worlds of his ancestors.*
— Edward T. Hall, *The Hidden Dimension*

AT DAWN, far away in the mist on a brown-red rocky ground, a man was coming from nowhere, his turban and his robe flapping in the wind. He was alone in the immensity of the horizon of African space.

I first encountered the desert when I was thirteen years old. My father had taken me to Sahara. It was then that I took my first pictures, with a Brownie flash, and it was then that the idea of becoming a photographer entered my mind.

The traveler — and even more so the photographer — is an observer. There is nothing extraordinary in the fact of traveling. The extraordinary thing is to make the decision to go. Wherever he goes, the photographer is in a state of perceptive awareness. Avoiding the spectacular, the pompous, he notices the unimportant moments that are in fact all-important. Unexpectedly, he finds himself a historian, geographer, or sociologist by means of this poetic and documentary observation.

Niger is the perfect country of initiation, called "Africa in Africa" by those who love the continent. From there I journeyed to southern Morocco, then along the Senegal River, the natural border between Senegal and Mauritania and the link between the desert and savanna, between the nomads and the forest people. Then to Egypt, where the pyramids of Meidum and Saqqara are sentinels to the rocky infinitude stretching to the Atlantic Ocean. Five thousand years of history are represented in that land, where the tribes coming from Judeo-Syria mixed with tribes already there, making from east to west the enormous ethnic group called the Hamitic nation.

Of all my journeys, Africa has been the farthest away in time. There I have escaped from my own century and my own time-fragmented culture to wander among the never-ending songs of the Peul Bororos, the Tuareg drums, the Guedra dance of the Moorish women, the sound of the Koran, the muezzin's call to prayer.

On the desert, the wind ceaselessly builds sand pyramids that disappear as fast as they form. The sand voluptuously infiltrates the people's veils and mirages float over the dry land.

But writing about the desert can fast become overly lyrical. One should not talk too much. That is what these huge spaces, this dust, these thorns, teach us — to stop speaking, at last.

Also, the reality of droughts, with the pain and suffering they bring, does not lend itself to poetic terms. There is no romance about rains that never fall, and there is no significance in beauty when food and water are desperately needed. And now that uranium has been found in this part of the world, things will change faster than you or I can imagine.

Photographic essays on worlds disappearing or changing are dramatic. Edward Curtis's pictures of American Indians are not merely beautiful; they also convey some of the tension of the fading nomadic freedom. The same is true of Wilfred Thesiger's photographs of Arabian desert nomads. But desert life persists, somehow, despite problems and dramas. And the wind erases the traces of tires on the sand . . . right away.

BERNARD PLOSSU

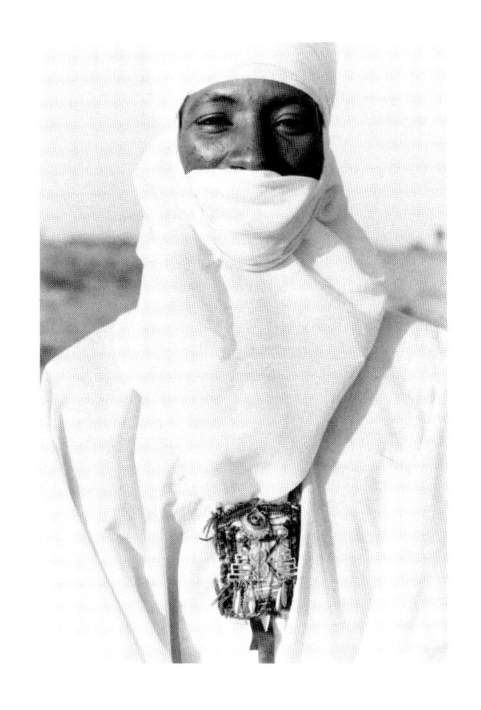

# Acknowledgments

I MADE THIS BOOK for my father, who crossed the Sahara in 1936, and for Shane, my son, born in the American desert.

All these photographs were taken in 1975, 1976, and 1977 with a 50mm lens on a Nikkormat camera.

Many thanks for their great help to Yveline Poncet and Moussa Hamidou; to Philippe Salaun for the prints; to James Enyeart and Terence Pitts of the Center for Creative Photography in Tucson, Arizona; and to Gilles Mora and Claude Nori of "Les cahiers de la photographie."

Meanwhile, Max Pam was continuing to photograph Asia.

Prints courtesy of the Eaton/Shoen Gallery in San Francisco.

# THE PHOTOGRAPHS

51

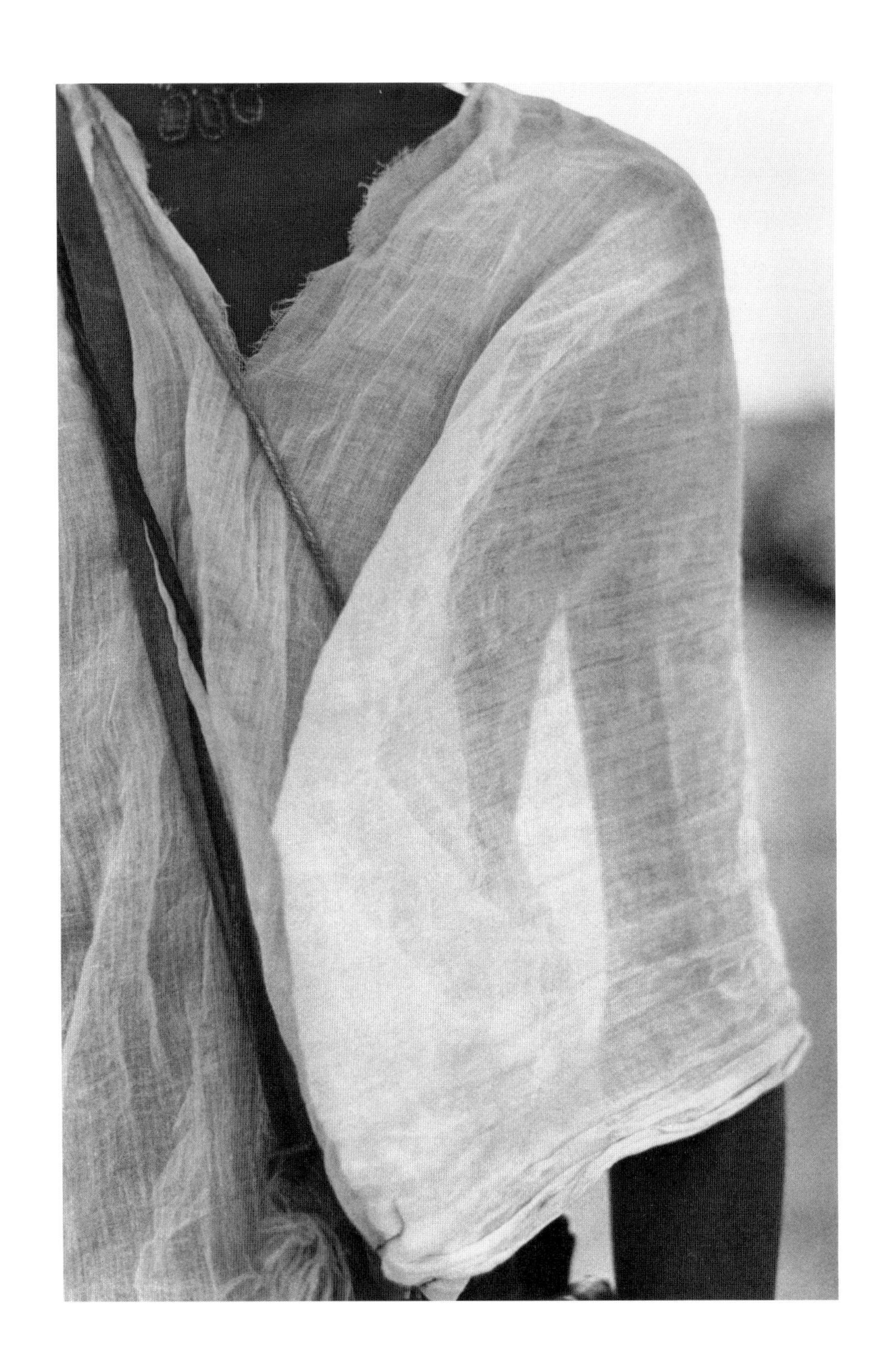

# The Photographs

61. The sleeping Mauritanian, Darou-Mousty, Senegal
62. Bororo Fulani nomad
63. Adobe walls around the mosque of Agadès, Niger
64. Adobe desert town in southern Morocco
65. Daughters of the Sultan of Agadès, Niger
66. Street in Agdz, southern Morocco
67. Afternoon shadows in Agadès, Niger
68. Moonrise over the Mosque of Agadès, Niger
69. Fulani Bororo nomads singing at moonrise, Agadès, Niger
71. Portrait of Bororo nomad at dusk, Niger
72. Mauritanian woman in the market, taking a break from the heat, Senegal
73. The tailor, Agadès, Niger
75. Two young nomad friends, Bororos, Niger
76. Three Tuaregs at dusk, Agadès, Niger
77. Morning heat, southern Egypt
78. Fighters of the sultan, Agadès, Niger
79. Street at dusk in Podor, Senegal
80. El Hadj Adamo Sall in Dagana, Senegal
81. Two patriarchs of the desert, Filingué, Niger
82. Midday, Senegal
83. Shade in Podor, Senegal
84. Tuareg resting in the shade, Filingué, Niger
85. Senegal River at Dagana
86. Adobe buildings, near Zagora, southern Morocco
87. A marabout in desert, southern Morocco
89. Young Tuareg woman, Agadès, Niger